Del Shores
monologues
for actresses of all ages

DEL SHORES

Currents & Tangents Press

Copyright © 2016 by Del Shores
All rights reserved.

No part of this book may be reproduced in any form or by any electronic or mechanical means, including information storage and retrieval systems, without written permission from the author, except for the use of brief quotations in a book review.

Published by Currents & Tangents Press
Dallas, Texas

CONTENTS

Dramatic Monologues-Female
Therapy Sessions

Voices   11
Age: Late Teens-20s

Aging Gracefully   12
Age: 50+

About Momma   13
Age: Late Teens-30s

About Daddy   14
Age: 20s-40s

The Millers   15
Age: Youth

The Towel   16
Age: 20s-40s

I Will Remember You   17
Age: Teens

Broken   18
Age: Teens

Fix Me   19
Age: Teens

Falling Out   20
Age: 20s-40s

Pretty Girl   21
Age: Teens

Closure   22
Age: 40s-70s

Late   23
Age: Teens

Lard Ass   24
Age: 20s-30s

Mom's In Rehab   25
Age: Teens

Served   26
Age: 30s-50s

Extract   27
Age: 30s-50s

Dramatic Monologues-Female
Phone Calls

Trained Professional   29
Age: 30s-50s

Tough Call   30
Age: 40s-50s

Homemade Pie   31
Age: Late 20s–early 40s

I'm Not You, Mom!   32
Age: Teens

Blood On My Car   33
Age: Late Teens-40s

Booze, Pills And Husbands   34
Age: 20s-50s

Facebook Notification   35
Late Teens-20s

The Call   36
Age: 30s-60s

Comedic Monologues-Female
Therapy Sessions

eHarmony   38
Age: 30s-60s

I'm Going To Kill Him   39
Age: 30s-40s

Truck Driving Polygamy   40
Age: 20s-40s

Half Alien   41
Age: 30s-50s

Caffeinated   42
Age: 20s-40s

Skanky Braid   43
Age: 20s-30s

Run, Girl, Run   44
Age: 20s-30s

Genius Alibi   45
Age: Teens

Black Enough   46
Age: 30s-40s

Getting Even   47
Age: 20s-30s

A Good Game Of Bridge   48
Age: 40s-50s

The Gift Of Therapy   49
Age: 30s-50s

Comedic Monologues-Female
Phone Calls

Love Story   51
Age: Teens-30s

Crank Calls   52
Age: 40s-70s

See You Sunday   53
Age: 20s-40s

Titty Flip   54
Age: 30s-50s

Cupcake And Muffin Top   55
Age: Teens

Home Cooked Disaster   56
Age: Late Teens-30s

There's Something About An Old Mary   57
Age: 30s-50s

Pauline Pitiful   58
Age: 30s-40s

Booty Call   59
Age: 30s-50s

Stole   61
Age: 40s-60s

Fourth Best Friend   63
Age: Youth-Teens

Long Distance   64
Age: 20s-30s

Naming Dead Frogs   65
Age: 40s+

About The Author   67

ACKNOWLEDGEMENTS

Special thanks to Jeff Chaffin, Nancy Chartier, Michele Condrey, Erica Coppage, Sharon Garrison, Daniel Foster, Mat Hayes, Suzanne Horne, Jake Kerr, Zoe Kerr, Linda McAlister, Sadie McGoodwin, McGhee Monteith, and all the actors who have taken the dialogue in this book and brought life to my characters.

INTRODUCTION

I love actors. I love writing for them. I love directing them. I love the magic that happens when an actor breathes life into my characters and my words, making them their own where you actually believe that the person who was once just a vision, a thought, words on paper – is now ALIVE.

A few years ago, I was asked to conduct an acting workshop in Dallas for Screen Actors Guild. I never thought of myself as a teacher, but quickly realized as this workshop led to others, that teaching for me was just directing.

As I got to know many of my talented students, I realized that there was a missing element in many of their careers. They did not have an acting reel, and if they did, they didn't have work and characters on the reel that really showed how amazing they were. So, they were not getting the auditions nor the work that was worthy of their talents.

I started providing a service to actors where I would write original monologues or scenes that would showcase their talents and give them that missing tool for getting auditions and ultimately getting work.

This book is the result of me writing many original monologues that I shot for reels, with a few from my unproduced work thrown in for good measure. I chose set-ups that were ripe for drama and comedy for many different types. This book consists of "Therapy Sessions" and "Phone Calls."

I hope you enjoy reading and performing these monologues. I hope that they give you opportunity to not just work on your craft, but to also showcase your talent and get you into acting companies, schools, universities, agencies to become a working actor.

Always remember to strive for the truth and trust your gut in your acting.

Prepare, prepare, prepare.

But don't forget to have fun!

Del Shores

Female Dramatic Monologues

Therapy Sessions

VOICES

Character: Casey
Age: Late teens-20s

Scene Synopsis: An UNSEEN THERAPIST listens to CASEY who hears voices and suffers from schizophrenia. The voices tell her to harm people she loves.

CASEY
... can you hear them?
(looks around)
Sometimes there's more than one, but right now, it's just Tara. She tells me what to do and if I don't—
(scared)
No! I won't! Stop saying that! I can't do that! No, Tara, please don't make me. Not again. NO! NO! I can't. Not my baby brother. I don't want to hurt him. Mom gets so mad. Please, no, Tara—

AGING GRACEFULLY

Character: Millie
Age: 50+

Scene Synopsis: An UNSEEN THERAPIST listens to Millie who is very upset as she discusses a day at the grocery store.

MILLIE

Yesterday I was at the grocery story, by myself and I couldn't find... well, I couldn't find the section where the laxatives were. And I was embarrassed to ask because... I don't know why... I guess I'm just feeling old, you know with this... but all people get bunched up, not just old people. But I finally gave up and grabbed some prunes and there was this young lady there, she worked there, and I whispered, "Honey, could you just tell me where the laxatives are?" Quietly. I said it quietly because I was embarrassed. And that girl rolled her eyes, because obviously, her job was something she did not like, and she yelled at this fella way down the aisle, "Hey, Justin, take this old lady to the laxatives!"
And they both busted out laughing.
(tears up)
This is what I've become. An old woman who gets laughed at because I'm constipated. I always wanted to age gracefully, but... it's not working out that way.

ABOUT MOMMA

Character: Kamille
Age: Late teens-30s

Scene Synopsis: An UNSEEN THERAPIST listens to KAMILLE, pretty and distraught, as she tells the truth for the first time.

KAMILLE

... what she doesn't know how to do is take responsibility for all the damage that she's caused. To me, to my sisters... to my poor Dad who had to raise us in chaos. She quotes all the bullshit that she's learned in A.A., like "Your journey is your journey and you must take it alone" and blah, blah, blah, blah, bullshit, blah! But this journey I'm on, this miserable journey I'm on is because of her! I never had a sober mother and I never knew if I'd get a hug or a slap. So, I'm done. No, I'm beyond done! And I'm so mad, but I don't know where to put the anger, the fire, the rage that just needs to erupt. I—
(pause, tears up as she confesses)
And sometimes I wish... I fantasize and imagine she's dead. And I wish that she had just died. That one of those times when she drove drunk that she would have just wrapped herself around a tree and hurt nobody but herself and by her dying... she would never be able to hurt me again. And I hate myself for wishing such a horrible thing on the person... on the person... who gave me life.

ABOUT DADDY

Character: Brittany
Age: 20s-40s

Scene Synopsis: An UNSEEN THERAPIST listens to BRITTANY, who is on the verge of tears.

BRITTANY
... and then I remembered. I remembered the abuse. And it wasn't sexual, no, nothing like that but—
(tears start)
All the memories kept flowing... all of them... from as far back as I can remember... where he told me that I wasn't smart enough... or pretty enough—or good enough... and I started... I started to believe that. Even when I was about to get married, the first time... we were about to walk down the aisle, you know, he was giving me away, which I thought he was thrilled to do, and he looked at me—and I thought he was going to say, I'm so happy for you or you look so pretty on your special day... but... no, he said, you are marrying way out of your league, young lady.
And I guess... no I did. I believed him.
(explodes)
Oh God, I just hate him! I hate him!

THE MILLERS

Character: Grace
Age: Youth

Scene Synopsis: An UNSEEN THERAPIST listens to GRACE who is a foster child in the system. She's wounded and vulnerable.

GRACE
(tears about to flow)
... but I liked the Millers. Why do I have to...? I just don't understand. Every night Mrs. Miller would brush my hair, one hundred times and kiss me good night. What did I do wrong?
(now crying)
What did I do wrong?
(then realizing)
They're not really going to keep Bobby and not me, are they?
(panicked)
Are they? Please, no, please don't let –
(breaks down, can't continue)

THE TOWEL

Character: Jennifer
Age: 20s - 40s

Scene Synopsis: An UNSEEN THERAPIST listens to JENNIFER who is already in tears, talking through the emotion.

JENNIFER

... and I was only fifteen years old. A preacher's daughter who had this horrible secret and nobody could know. Nobody. But... I was told about... this woman, who did that. Got rid of it for you. My friend Janie loaned me the money, one hundred dollars, I don't know where she got it, but she had a license and drove me out to this trailer right outside of town. There were no drugs, nothing was sterile, nothing... just... so nasty...
(can barely talk)
...and she just ripped my insides out and took... my baby. I looked away, but after... after... I looked over and there was a towel covering this dirty, bloody wash basin and... and a tiny little hand was just peaking out.
(pause)
And that's what I see in the dreams, the nightmares—and I just don't think they'll ever go away. And I can't tell him. I can't tell anybody.

I WILL REMEMBER YOU

Character: Delaney
Age: Teens

Scene Synopsis: An UNSEEN THERAPIST listens to DELANEY who is already in tears.

DELANEY
(quietly)
I didn't want to, but he... he told me that if I didn't there are plenty of girls that would and... I liked him. So, I closed my eyes and... just let him. And it hurt...at first, but I just blocked everything out and started singing in my head... this Sara McLaughlin song, "I will remember you, will you remember me?" My mom always listens to that song and it's, you know... soothing... And then it was over and I thought, you got what you wanted and I've messed up and now he'll dump me and just move on, because he's a player. Everybody warned me, but... I like him but.. That's exactly what he did. And he started ignoring my texts... and me at school—
(pause)
And I'm late. I've never been late before. And I'm so scared.

BROKEN

Character: Alexa
Age: Teens

Scene Synopsis: An UNSEEN THERAPIST listens to ALEXA, a very troubled teen, whose eyes already are glistening with tears.

ALEXA
So, no, I don't want to be here because I can't be fixed! She wants me here so I'll get better and it won't, I won't remind her—
(pause, tears)
Of what she did. And whether she believes that she did it or not, she did because she married him knowing…there were others. He was registered, okay, and now I know that she knew, so yeah, she allowed it to happen. For all those years. And I just can't get better because he broke something that can't be fixed and—
(sudden anger)
She admitted she knew—so she's just going to have to live with the guilt!

FIX ME

Character: Becca
Age: Youth/Teens

Scene Synopsis: An UNSEEN THERAPIST listens to BECCA, an angry girl who has been forced by her parents to go to therapy.

BECCA
(silence, attitude)
So, are we going to just sit here and stare at each other like monkeys at the zoo or what... because...
(angry, yelling)
I DO NOT WANT TO BE HERE!
(laughs)
Ha! Made you flinch! So—
(more silence, then tone change, leans forward)
Look, I don't want to be the bad kid... and don't tell my Dad, but if you... I will try and figure this out if...
(tears fill her eyes)
If you can fix me. Because everybody else has given up on me.

FALLING OUT

Character: Christina
Age: 20s-40s

Scene Synopsis: An UNSEEN THERAPIST listens to CHRISTINA as she talks about how she's dealing with her cancer treatment. She slides her hand through her hair.

CHRISTINA

Look, it's falling out. They told me that it probably... that most likely, it wouldn't fall out, that I wouldn't lose my hair. And now...
(tears up)
... it's just such a reminder, you know. I sometimes fall asleep, this really deep sleep, and when I wake up, I don't know if it's the drugs—or cancer. But I can't wake up like I used to and I'm kinda awake, but not really and my mind floats to this pool of water under a waterfall in Hawaii that I went to with my parents on vacation when I was like eight or nine. And I'm laughing and happy again... then, I start waking up and I realize that I'm really sick because I see the hair on my pillow—and I'm just so scared.

PRETTY GIRL

Character: Teanna
Age: Teens

Scene Synopsis: An UNSEEN THERAPIST listens to TEANNA, an angry, upset, cutter. She sits with her arms crossed, long sleeves, with extreme attitude.

TEANNA

Then why don't you ask her what she does to make me like this!? You think I want to be the screwed up girl, the one that everybody at school points at and laughs and calls "Scar Girl"—
(almost pleading)
I just want to feel. Anything. And I can't feel. Mom... Mother... always says, "you're the pretty girl". But I don't feel pretty... ever... I just feel invisible. So, why don't you ask my mother what she did to make me feel nothing?
(softly)
I just want to feel.

CLOSURE

Character: Louisa
Age: 40s-70s

Scene Synopsis: An UNSEEN THERAPIST listens to LOUISA, who is already emotional. She looks at her therapist, then away, then back again.

LOUISA

It would have been easier if he had... oh, I know I shouldn't say this... but it would have been easier if he had...
(deep breath, pushing through emotion)
... died. I could have had closure, you know? It's... well, eight weeks now. One day you wake up, he's next to you, the next day, you wake up—alone. But for that one split second, before reality hits, you wake up thinking that everything is okay, the way it was, the way it should be. And then... then you remember. And you start your day just confused and hurt and... feeling old, used and disposed of. And you just lay there because you can't get up and... yes, death... well, you would have at least found closure.
(softly)
I don't know how to find closure.

LATE

Character: Avery
Age: Teens

Scene Synopsis: An UNSEEN THERAPIST listens to AVERY, who is already in tears, a pillow covering her stomach.

AVERY

I swear, it was just that one time. And it wasn't my fault. I... okay, yeah, I drank too much and... well, there had to be something they put in my drink because I don't remember. Anything.
(hard to continue)
... when I woke up I was... I was there with like three guys... I don't know what happened. So, I got dressed and... how am I going to tell my parents? I'm three months late. I don't know... who... do I have to tell them? Please, help me...
(sobbing)
They're going to be so disappointed.

LARD ASS

Character: Whitney
Age: 20s-30s

Scene Synopsis: An UNSEEN THERAPIST listens to WHITNEY, pretty and smug.

WHITNEY

I saw this guy.. Danny Hopkins... he was a football player in high school, really cute and popular. He was the one I told you about, you know, he and all his friends would bully me, call me "lard ass", "Carny Wilson"...that kinda stuff. And he was standing at the bar—at Mexicali—and our eyes met. I know, I know, but I thought, yeah, it's pay back time. Once he and his goons surrounded me by the lockers after school and were harassing me and one of them said, "Hey Danny, you need to...
(gets emotional)
... to pity "f" her. And I was crying and he said, "Well, I'd have to dip her in flour first to find the wet spot."
(smiles)
So, I ordered some coffee, then walked over slowly, you know, sexy and said, "I bet you want to get naked with me and do really nasty things."
And he smiled and said, "Well, that's certainly a good start." So I reached down and put my hand down his pants and said, "I'm Whitney Reese" also known as "lard ass" or "Carny Wilson", ring a bell? And he said, "Wow, you have lost a shit ton of weight. Then I poured the scalding hot coffee down his pants and walked right out of that bar while he was screaming and yelling, "You bitch, you bitch!"
(laughs, then mood change)
But... when I got home, I looked in the mirror and... I saw a fat girl staring back at me. And I just don't know if that will ever change.

MOM'S IN REHAB

Character: Kelly
Age: Teens

Scene Synopsis: An UNSEEN THERAPIST listens to KELLY, who is blaming herself because her mom is back in rehab.

KELLY

... we had this great visit, finally, Dad let me see her, and she told me... she told me, "you're the reason I stay sober. You're the reason I stay alive." And it was like... for the first time, she was being a Mom. She paid for pizza and bought me an outfit... but... she two days later she called me slurring and said she had taken cold medicine when I confronted her. She thinks I'm stupid, like after all these years, she can fool me.
(tears)
So, now she's back... in rehab, again. And I was wondering, why I wasn't enough for her... enough for her to stay sober.
(pause)
And sometimes, I have nightmares that she kills herself... and I wasn't enough... just wasn't enough.

SERVED

Character: Deborah
Age: 30s-50s

Scene Synopsis: An UNSEEN THERAPIST listens to DEBORAH who stares for a second, somewhere between anger and distraught, before she speaks.

DEBORAH

... so I met him in a park because I did not want to meet in a restaurant, you know, in case, someone I knew was there or... okay, in case it got heated and I started crying. And he handled me the divorce papers to look over, said I'd be "served" next week. And they were fine, simple... everything we had agreed on... you know, clean. The perfect tidy ending to the mess he had left me in.
(pause, fighting tears)
And I looked at him and said, "Ron, I never want to see you again. I never want to hear from you again. No texts! No emails! Nothing!" He nodded... like, you know... whatever, almost like I was doing him a favor. And I said, "You do know that you are a despicable human being!? The way you did this! Leaving me... In chaos!
(anger building)
Just blind siding me?! No warning! No hint! Nothing!!
(pause)
And you know what he said? He said, "I did the best I could." And I just looked at him and said, "Well, that's the shittiest best I've ever witnessed."
(tone change, emotional)
I'm lost. I'm just lost now... lost.

EXTRACT

Character: Tina
Age: 30s-50s

Scene Synopsis: An UNSEEN THERAPIST listens to a very upset, tearful TINA.

TINA

It's just like a chromosome or something... like a piece of your fabric, your DNA, your make-up, you know... that you just can't extract. And I so desperately want to extract and forget all those voices, those sermons that told me that... that I was not worthy of God's love. And when you hear these things from your own parents... from your strict preacher Daddy and your sweet, sweet Sunday-school teaching Christian Mama who meant no harm, but... they both didn't... it just won't go away. Ever since the baby... when I got pregnant... I was only fifteen and oh, God, that awful girl's home they sent me to, where every day you heard what a worthless sinner you were and they made you beg for forgiveness over and over... and if you didn't, you got licks, a belt that would leave whelps. And then, you... I... was forced... to leave my baby... and, I have regrets, but... and I want to.. You know rid myself of all that damage. But it's there... and I hear the sermons and see the pulpit and my daddy screaming hell, fire and brimstone... and I don't feel worthy of God's love, and I don't think I ever will. Ever.

Female Dramatic Monologues

Phone Calls

TRAINED PROFESSIONAL

Character: Dr. Rachel Reeves
Age: 30s-50s

Scene Synopsis: DR. RACHEL REEVES, a therapist, sits on the couch of her office. She talks on the phone, close to, or in tears.

RACHEL

I'm so sick of you lying, Dan... ! I'm a trained professional, goddamnit, I know you when you are lying. You get that lower tone and your voice starts quivering and you keep saying, "I'm not lying, I'm not lying." If you aren't lying, you don't have to say it! And a liar doesn't call every time they are missing and their cell phone goes right to voice mail for hours at a time... so, just say it, Dan. Just fucking say that you're a goddamn, cheatin' asshole lying sack of shit.
(There is a KNOCK on the door.)
Okay, fine, I've got to go. I have a patient.
(covers phone)
Just a moment.
(back in phone)
We are not done with this. Not even close!

TOUGH CALL

Character: Lee
Age: 40s – 50s

Scene Synopsis: LEE is on the phone, very upset. We catch her in mid-story, fighting tears – and losing.

                              LEE
I just never thought that … I just never thought that I was that type of person. To abandon my own Mama. I love her so much, but… I'm fried… and ill-equipped and I kept telling myself—no, this is right. It's a great home. Doctors are there, nurses… round the clock care and she's better off because if something happens here while I'm gone or can't …
                           (pause)
But in my heart, all I wonder is… what is she going to think when the daughter she raised and cared for… and loved… just puts her away… leaves her own sweet mama… there… to die.

HOMEMADE PIE

Character: Michele
Age: Late 20s – early 40s

Scene Synopsis: MICHELE is a frazzled, hot mess, trying to whip eggs into meringue.

MICHELE
I'm trying, Mother! I'm beating as fast I can. Maybe if you had taught me to cook—
(pause)
Okay, bake then, I stand corrected, well, maybe if you had taught me to bake instead of... oh, I don't know, drinking a bottle of wine every night of my childhood, I'd be more equipped to take something homemade to the band bake sale!
(yells)
Jacob, Miranda, Brenda! We have to leave right now so I can stop by the bakery to buy a pie because Grandma was too drunk to teach me how to make a lemon meringue pie! Hold on, Mother!
(clicks over to other line)
Hello. Bill I can't talk right now!
(listens)
I can't talk right now! I can't talk right now!
(hangs up and bursts into tears)

I'M NOT YOU, MOM!

Character: Caroline
Age: Teens

Scene Synopis: CAROLINE is talking to her Mom on her cellphone, upset, on the verge of a meltdown.

CAROLINE
... I need you to pick me up now outside the gym.
(bursts into tears)
Because I already got cut! You said I could do anything I wanted, Mom. Anything. Anything? Really? Because I wanted to be cheerleader and I didn't make it. Again. My last chance. Maybe you should have said, "Caroline, you can be anything in life—except a cheerleader!" "Go for it. Try out! Believe it! Achieve it! Well, guess what Mother—?
(softer chokes up)
I'm not that girl. I'm not like you were. Not that perfect, skinny, popular girl—and I know that disappoints you, but I never will be. I'm just... me. So I've got to figure out a way to be okay with that and not disappointing you.

BLOOD ON MY CAR

Character: Janet
Age: Late Teens – 40s

Scene Synopsis: JANET is on the phone, on the verge of hysteria. She looks trashed, as if she stayed up all night, still in party clothes.

JANET
Madie, it's me. Oh my God, no... I don't... I don't know what to do.
(listens)
Yes, something is terribly wrong. I... It's all over the news and I just remembered... I woke up and I turned on the news... I drank too much at Ronnie's party and I don't even remember getting home, but... I... I remembered hitting her. That girl... Stephanie. She was at the party and the news says she's in intensive care and they're looking for... they're looking for me, Madie.
(breaking down)
I hit her! I don't remember anything else, but I remember it so clear... she walked right out in front of me and I couldn't stop in time... and I panicked and just... I guess I drove all the way home and passed out. There's blood on my car. I checked and... I've ruined my life... and she may die—
(crying)
Oh God—

BOOZE, PILLS AND HUSBANDS

Character: Marion
Age: 20s – 50s

Scene Synopsis: MARION, drunk and on pills, make-up smeared, hair a mess, wearing a very expensive silk robe trimmed in feathers of some sort pours another drink. She picks up the phone, dials and waits for an answer.

MARION

Mama?! It's your wayward daughter. I want to know something. Are you proud of me?
(laughs, then gets emotional)
Five husbands and I killed them all! I did. I drove every last one of them to their miserable graves. You said, "Marion, it's just as easy to love a rich man than to love a poor man." Well, I did it! And now... I have everything! Everything!
(looks around)
Except a goddamn cork screw. How the hell am I gonna chase down my Oxycontin with a good, classy wine that shows... style and upbringing if I don't have a FUCKING corkscrew!? Mama!? Mama!? Don't you dare hang up on me!
(pause)
She hung up on me.

FACEBOOK NOTIFICATION

Character: Lacy
Age: Late Teen – 20s

Scene Synopsis: LACY is reading a computer screen on the phone.

LACY
I broke into his Facebook and am at his messages. Oh no! There's a message here for someone named Catherine. Oh shit! Oh shit! He's cheatin' on me with someone name Catherine! I bet she has money. Nobody names their kid Catherine who doesn't have money.
(reads)
Oh God, Shay, he is. He is. I've got the proof now. It's dirty. It's real dirty. She wrote nasty shit about his big dick! Big!? Big! His dick not all that big. It's average. Barely! This Catherine is a rich, trash talkin' whorebag liar!

THE CALL

Character: Beth
Age: 30s – 60s

Scene Synopsis: BETH pours a glass of wine. The phone rings.

BETH
Hello. Yes, this is Beth Daniels.
Yes, yes, that's my husband. David Daniels. What... why... is there something wrong.
(listens, horror on face)
Oh, no. Is he—? Okay, okay. No, but I can drive over. Yes, I'm—Just... oh God, please... just tell him to... Tell him I love him and—that Bethie loves him and I'll there as soon as I can.
(crying)
Yes, okay, of course. I'm on my way—

Female Comedy Monologues

Therapy Sessions

eHARMONY

Character: Sue Ellen
Age: 30s-60s

Scene Synopsis: An UNSEEN THERAPIST listens to SUE ELLEN, who is on a rant!

SUE ELLEN

... so yes, at my age and after divorce, I'm trying to date and frankly, I just don't know how. So, yes, I took your advice and joined eHarmony, but this article I read... it just, well, messed me up. It was about a woman who sat on her toilet for two years because she had agoraphobia. Ultimately, her hiney fused to the seat and they had to take her to the ER with the toilet seat attached to it. Talk about humiliating! But you know what the kicker was—she had a boyfriend! A boyfriend who would bring her food so she could stay holed up in her bathroom with a toilet seat stuck to her ass. Thanks to your brilliant suggestion, I have now had five dates on eHarmony and I'm obviously so pathetic, the only men interested in me have more hair in their ears than on their head and use Groupons. Who uses Groupons—on your first date? Cheap-ass dates you find on eHarmony, that's who! Yet, Commode Lady has a boyfriend!
(looks away, tears fill her eyes)
I miss him. I never thought... and sometimes, I wake up... alone... and I can't get out of bed for the longest time and I wonder... what did I do wrong? Why wasn't I enough...

I'M GOING TO KILL HIM

Character: Randi
Age: 30s-40

Scene Synopsis: An UNSEEN THERAPIST listens to RANDI who has plenty of attitude, is somewhat bitter and is already heated.

RANDI

I want to kill him, okay? Okay, not really because I know you guys have to report that shit and if I'm going to murder him or hurt myself, then I better keep it to myself here. Okay, I'm not going to do either, so get over it. But I couldn't stop eating! I was PMSing, okay? And he called me a fat ass! Yeah, and then he said he wasn't physically attracted to me anymore! And I'm like, really? Because with that gut, you look like you're about four months pregnant, no, make that five! And what's up with guys anyway? They can get fat and scratch their balls like we can't see that—but they want their women perfect! He's such a douche bag.

TRUCK DRIVING POLYGOMY

Character: Lori
Age: 20s - 40s

Scene Synopsis: An UNSEEN THERAPIST listens to LORI who is a pissed-off, betrayed motor-mouth betrayed wife.

LORI
... and there are all these emails between some skank in Roswell, New Mexico. See, this is the problem with long-haul truck drivers, I swore I'd never date one again, but he had that thing... frankly that big thing... and that smile. Three dimples. Oh my God, when he smiles, I just melt.
(suddenly realizing)
Oh my God! What if he's married to her!? Diedra. That's her name. What if he has a complete other family with Diedra from Roswell, New Mexico and I'm part of some truck-drivin' polygamy crap and unlike that show "Big Love", which I don't really like, I'm not in on it! He's not even a Mormon for crissakes!

HALF ALIEN

Character: Pat
Age: 30s-50s

Scene Synopsis: An UNSEEN THERAPIST listens to PAT, who wrings her hands, bat-shit crazy, eyes darting around as if someone is after her.

PAT
... and if you don't think that there is a conspiracy going on you are sadly mistaken. Yes, there are aliens, but they are as much a part of this administration as Hilary Clinton is. Obama is half alien, not half black. They breed with us, you know. Aliens. I'm living proof. It happened to me July 18th 1987. I was taken into one of their capsules and they raped me—
(this is hard, emotional)
They raped me, repeatedly, and yes, I conceived, I know you were wondering, I'm a little bit psychic too. I lost my half-alien baby. But I was far enough along that he had a face.
(leans in, very hush-hush)
And he looked exactly like Barack Obama. Only smaller.

CAFFEINATED

Character: Mary
Age: 20s-40s

Scene Synopsis: An UNSEEN THERAPIST listens to MARY'S session right after the death of her sister. She is highly caffeinated.

MARY
(rapid fire)
Look, I'm just going to warn you, I'm really jacked up on caffeine and yeah, well, I sat at Starbucks for like three hours before our sessions because I can't fucking drink anymore, thank you Judge Jackson! And I'm upset, okay!? Three shots per cappuccino's, I ordered an extra, and this is number two, plus a double shot of espresso, so whew, I'm speedy, okay? Eight shots.
(a breath, trying to compose)
My sister, as you know, killed herself last week and she left that fucking note that said I wasn't a good sister—like ever—because I stole some guy—Billy Dobson—from her, in tenth grade, who is now fat and bald and dead. Well, I guess he's not fat and bald anymore, but he was, you know, before his death, which was caused I'm sure by his red meat diet. But the point is I was a great fucking sister and she was the horrible sister—and I can't cry, okay, for her because I'm so pissed and it's expected—
(pause)
And maybe she doesn't deserve my tears.

SKANKY BRAID

Character: Ashley
Age: 20s-30s

Scene Synopsis: An UNSEEN THERAPIST listens to ASHLEY who's is in the middle of a well-earned rant.

ASHLEY

So he said, "I love you baby" and I was waiting for that okay, and I was ready to strike and I said, "Well if you love me, then what was this braid doing under your bed?!" And I pulled it out of my purse when I said the word, "bed". I dropped an earring and looked under the bed and found this skanky braid, okay? And he was like...
(imitating him)
"Uh, I don't know, um, um, um, um, oh that's the maid's braid" and I said, "You don't have no maid, Rodney" and he laughed and said, "I'm just kiddin' baby, but what he was doing was stallin', trying to come up with a good excuse. And you know what his good excuse was? "Oh, I know whose braid that is, it's my ex ex girlfriend Brandy's." He dated Brandy like four years ago and I said, "You hadn't cleaned under your bed for four years? You do need a maid!"
(mood change)
But I gave him another chance, knowing he cheated on me again! What is wrong with me?

RUN, GIRL, RUN

Character: Shannon
Age: 20s-30s

Scene Synopsis: An UNSEEN THERAPIST listens to SHANNON, who is dressed to the nines.

SHANNON

What the hell is wrong with me! Another one turned out gay! So I called Dave, my gay ex-husband, and said, you have to help me, because I can't go through this again. Roger, that's the new guy's name, invited me over for dinner. So, the plan was for me to call Dave and describe his apartment after I got there. So, I snuck into the bathroom to call and EVERYTHING was so neat and perfect and matching and orderly. Great hand towels... oh, and there was even a triangle folded at the end of the toilet paper like at a hotel! So, I called Dave and I said, "I'm staring at potpourri, towels that <u>match</u> the dried roses in the potpourri and before I said another word, Dave blurted out, "Run, girl, run!"
(laughs)
So... so I said I have explosive diarrhea and ran! Best excuse ever!

GENIUS ALIBI

Character: Chloe
Age: Teens

Scene Synopsis: An UNSEEN THERAPIST listens to CHLOE who is in the throes of a confession.

CHLOE

So, I found out that he... Devin... hooked up with my former best friend Andi at this party last week! Everybody saw them together and I was home with the flu, okay? So, I thought, like, okay you asked for it. So I took some lighter fluid and matches and right in the middle of gym class, I snuck out and nobody even knew, and I set his locker on fire –
(laughs)
... and get this, his favorite hoodie, the Abercrombie one that I gave him for Christmas was in there. I went behind the gym, hid the lighter fluid in the trash bin under a pile of leaves and then went back in and ran laps and nobody ever even knew I was gone! Genius alibi!
(off therapist look; intense, disturbing)
He cheated on me and he deserved it! Don't act like I did something wrong!
(beat)
You don't have to report this, do you?

BLACK ENOUGH

Character: Shalitras
Age: 30s-40s

Scene Synopsis: An UNSEEN THERAPIST listens to SHALITRAS – African American, arms crossed – who tries to make sense of her life.

SHALITRAS

I'm tired of people expecting me to talk, act and be – blacker. This is 2012, people, we are not in "The Help"! We have moved forward, thank God almighty. But, see, I'm nervous as hell after turning in my first draft, and my publisher reads it and sets a meeting. And she says, "You're writing a girl from the projects who has risen above, succeeded." Yeah, I know, I've written me, so I know how to write for me! And she says I need to make her more "urban", "more ghetto if you will!" And I'm messing with her and say I don't understand and she says, "Oh for crissakes, make her blacker!" Look at me! Am I black enough?
(she laughs)
So I open my book and point to some dialogue and say, "So this part would be better if she said, "Hey girl...
(then pissed)
... Oh no you didn't! Uh, uh, no, you didn't! You talkin' to the hand now, girl!" And she said, "Exactly!"
(pause)
Seriously? Exactly?
(then screaming)
I'm about to lose my freakin' mind here!

GETTING EVEN

Character: Lucinda
Age: 20s-30s

Scene Synopsis: An UNSEEN THERAPIST listens to LUCINDA talking to a mile a minute. It's hard to follow her trail of crumbs.

LUCINDA

... well, so, see, Tiffany Bradford is a bitch and yeah I'm a bitch too, well, I can be, not always, but sometimes – but I'm not the kind of bitch that would cheat with my friend's boyfriend, even if, you know, well, there was an incident and yeah, I think she was getting even, and maybe he was too, because, okay, yes, there was another incident and somebody did pee all over his Range Rover, and okay, I didn't do it, cause it's easier for a guy, to, you know aim, but I... Okay, I had my friend Ronnie Gonzales do it, the peeing, gave him twenty dollars, BUT in my defense, Hunter forgot our anniversary! I sent him balloons with a cute chimpanzee holding the balloons 'cause he likes monkeys and I guess the card fell off 'cause he called and said, "What's this for?" He totally forgot our six-month anniversary! So, yes, I paid Ronnie to pee in his Range Rover, and as for Tiffany, yes, I did throw a shoe at her at Bar Centrale, but ask anybody, she deserved it and that does NOT give you the right to make out with my boyfriend!

A GOOD GAME OF BRIDGE

Character: Billie
Age: 40s-50s

Scene Synopsis: An UNSEEN THERAPIST listens to BILLIE, upscale and social. SHE frustrated and upset.

BILLIE

Look, the truth of the matter is… I hate her! I simply loathe Abigail Kirkpatrick. She is a passive, aggressive bitch. There I said it. If I could kick her out of our bridge club, I would, but I can't because her husband is my husband's boss. And she knows that, so that's the reason she has chosen me as her punching bag. You know what she said at last week's game. As I was eating a piece of chocolate, okay my third piece, and she said, "Oh I wish I could just pop chocolates in my mouth like Billie here and not care about the size of my derriere!" My "derriere" is not big, thank you very much! It is the perfect size! So, I'm helpless, bound… unless… unless I put some Visine in her drink. That's an old flight attendant trick to stop drunks from drinking. Causes instant diarrhea!
(thinks)
But I'll have to wait until towards the end of the game.
(off therapist's looks)
Well, you don't want to mess up a good game of bridge!

THE GIFT OF THERAPY

Character: Lisa
Age: 30s-50s

Scene Synopsis: An UNSEEN THERAPIST listens to LISA, a Texas waitress. This is her first session.

LISA

Well, I'll just say right here and now that I do not need you! But my husband gave me this therapy session for a Christmas present and said he would leave me if I didn't come to it. So, here I am and frankly I would have much preferred the cash! And yes, I've been in a bad mood since last August and Bud is not used to me actin' ugly all the time, but I can't shake this! I just can't. And it's all because of that illegal alien's death! That busboy who took them diet pills from China and died in his sleep.
(very serious)
Don't take diet pills from China you buy off the internet! Big lesson for us all. And yes, I could have been more sympathetic, but I do not believe that I deserved to be fired over being insensitive over an illegal alien's death! His name was Adrian Duarte. And I would have been more sensitive if he had been nicer to me when he bused my tables – when he was alive. Called me a –
(whispers)
"puta" once – that means "prostitute" in Spanish! Whore! He said he didn't but I heard him plain and clear after I told him he missed a big glob of mustard after he wiped down the bar. And all I said was, "I don't know why everybody's so sad over an illegal alien's death who was only part time and should have known better than to take diet pills from China." So, if that was insensitive, sue me!
(glares at therapist, then erupts)
And I don't need you!

Female Comedy Monologues

Phone Calls

LOVE STORY

Character: Jenny
Age: Teens-30s

Scene Synopsis: JENNY, in sweats and t-shirt, eats ice cream and is watching "Love Story"; she is crying.

JENNY

Oh no! Don't die! Cure her, damnit! Cancer is so... mean.
(Picks up her cell phone and talks through tears)
Deana? When I said I wanted you to recommend an old movie that was a love story, I meant a happy love story! And that title—"Love Story" is just so wrong! It's deceptive is what it is! Love story makes you think it's happy... and this is beyond sad! It needs to be called, oh I don't know, "College Cancer" or something. And here's another thing, "love means never having to say you're sorry"? Really? What if you step on his toe or bleach his favorite shirt? And what about, well, like that time Will farted during sex... sorry is the right thing to say! I gotta go, she's about to die.
(hangs up and starts crying again.)

CRANK CALLS

Character: Ethel
Age: 40s-70s

Scene Synopsis: ETHEL, a sweet Christian, is on the phone.

ETHEL
... so I just smiled weakly and told her that her hair looked just fine, but honey, she is livin' proof that home perms do not work! Hold on, Delores.
(answers phone)
Hello.
(listens)
I'm sorry, but Pastor is out visiting the elderly and afflicted tonight. I'll tell him you called. Bye, now.
(back to Delores)
That was poor old Widow Walker. She calls every night... bless her heart. Hold on.
(answers another line)
Hello... now you stop callin' here! I do not like crank calls. I mean it!
(back to Delores)
It was that crank caller again. Asked me if I was wearin' any...
(whispers)
... panties. Satan is at work, Delores. Alive and well in Marfa, Texas, no doubt in my mind. Hold on.
(answers other line)
Hello... Listen you little sinner, stop callin' here, I'm about to have this phone tapped by the F.B.I.!
(back to Delores)
It was that crank caller... he's making me a nervous wreck... hold on.
(answers)
Hello... listen you little asshole...!

SEE YOU SUNDAY

Character: Natalie
Age: 20s-40s

Scene Synopsis: NATALIE, pissed, holds her phone, thinks, then dials.

NATALIE

Hello, yes Shannon, this is Natalie. Put your asshole husband on, will ya?
(listens)
Damn right, I'm mad. Good guess. Okay, thanks.
(waits)
Matt? Yeah, well, she's wrong. I'm not pissed, I'm beyond pissed. Now you shut up. I called and I'm gonna be doing the talkin'! Don't you ever call my son again and talk to him like you were his Daddy. I am his mother and his bastard dad left us high and dry and I've done very well all by myself, thank you very much.
(listens)
Oh really? Well, I don't give a good goddamn if you think you had the right because you are the world's greatest dad, a deacon down at the church or what the hell ever… that does not give you the right to parent my kid!
(short pause)
I said shut the hell up 'til I'm done. I'm doing the talking here, you're doing the listening, okay? Perhaps, Matt, your good little girl is not so good. Perhaps it's not Aaron leading her down the wrong road, but perhaps, just perhaps, she took him down that long and winding road – that's a Biblical reference in case you missed it – and perhaps, your little tramp is the one corrupting my son. So, get off your high and mighty high horse, Matt, because there is a reason your perfect little Casey has earned her reputation and has been given the nickname "Miss Peanut Butter Legs"—you know, easy to spread! So lay off my boy and I mean it! See you in church on Sunday. Bye now.
(hangs up, smiles)

TITTY FLIP

Character: Regina
Age: 30s-50s

Scene Synopsis: REGINA LEWIS, a former Miss Texas—or at least a fourth runner up is on the phone, in mid conversation.

REGINA
(laughing)
Oh Lord, stop! Stop! I had forgotten all about that. Yes! Miss Tennessee. 1978 or nine. Jovina Armstrong was her name. That is NOT a good name. That poor ol' gal wore that low-cut homemade gown that her mama made – that was when that was acceptable – and she started poundin' on that piano singing that gospel number "He". That's when we had real talent in the contest! Beauty and talent and no brains. Worked so much better. Well, she got all worked up and right as she got to "Though it makes Him sad to see the way we live" she started pounded those keys harder and her titty fell out!
(laughing more)
Fell right out and without missing a note, Jovina flipped that titty back in that gown and brought it on home, with "He'll always say, I forgive." And she won! I do believe that the mixture of religion and sexuality was just too much for those good ol' Southern boy judges to dismiss.

CUPCAKE AND MUFFIN TOP

Character: Kaylie
Age: Teens

Scene Synopsis: KAYLIE is on the phone with a girlfriend, opening a Glad container.

KAYLIE
... yeah, I made him his favorite cupcake and put a heart on the top, it's so cute... oh, my God, I forgot to tell you, Tea Jacobson was wearing skinny jeans with her big ol' muffin top hanging over them today and she bent over and you could see total butt crack, so gross –
(opens the Glad container, screams)
AHHH, someone at the cupcake and left like one bite! I'll call you back!
(calling)
Mom!
(bursts into tears)
Somebody, and I'm sure it was Tommy, ate the cupcake I made for Jared's birthday, his favorite cupcake... MOTHER!!!! GET DOWN HER NOW because my life just officially ended!!!

HOME COOKED DISASTER

Character: Amanda
Age: Late Teens – 30s

Scene Synopsis: AMANDA is on the phone with her friend, as she tries to prepare "dinner" for her date.

> AMANDA
> Yes, I have onions sautéing just
> like you said and the place smells
> so good. Oh, Luci, he is so cute and if I can just... I don't know, I just
> want him to like me! So, I stopped by Whole Foods and got rosemary
> chicken, mashed sweet potatoes and a salad.

She works with the containers, putting the food into bowls. She opens the chicken (covered by one of those hot food foil bags), pulls out the container and SCREAMS.

> AMANDA (CONT'D)
> Oh no! Oh no! There's nothing in
> the chicken container but bones! Somebody ate the entire chicken
> and just left the bones! Shit! Shit! Shit! What I'm I going to do?! I'm so
> screwed!
> (sniff, then turns)
> Shit!!! The onions are burning!

THERE'S SOMETHING ABOUT AN OLD MARY

Character: Gretchen
Age: 30s – 50s

Scene Synopsis: GRETCHEN has on a veil and a performance dress and is holding a child's doll in swaddling clothes. She is NOT all there!

GRETCHEN
(back to audience, deep voice)
Ladies and gentlemen, we welcome back to Carnegie Hall—the one, the only, GRETCHEN ROLLINS!
(turns around, smiles, taking in audience)
Oh, thank you. Thank you ever so much. It's so good to be back at Carnegie Hall. Christmas is my favorite time of year because of...
(chokes up)
Baby Jesus!
(sings)
"Away in a manager, no crib for a bed.
(phone rings)
The little Lord..."
(answers the phone)
Hello. Oh, hello Pastor Peake.
(listens)
Oh my goodness. Oh my goodness. Oh my goodness gracious alive!
(listens, very upset)
What!? Well, I never! I am insulted! Highly insulted! Just because the committee replaced the biggest star to come out of Concho County - ME - with that borderline ugly 17-year-old alleged virgin Tiffany Rodgers to play Mary – a roll I have played twenty-two years in a row – would not cause me to break the eight commandment and steal the baby Jesus! HOW DARE YOU!
(listens)
Oh. Well, you know I had forgotten all about those new surveillance cameras. I'll bring him right back!

PAULINE PITIFUL

Character: Pauline
Age: 30s – 40s

Scene Synopsis: PAULINE punches on her cell, very pissed off!

PAULINE

Yeah, hello, Morgana Wilson? Yeah, Pauline Rodgers. Taft High. We were polar opposites and now I'm back in town and you've been talking trash about me.
(pause)
Uh-huh? Really? Because I heard that you've been referring to me by my high school nickname "Pauline Pitiful." Yeah, ha, ha, ha! Well, that was then and this is now and in case you haven't heard, I'm still Pauline, but I'm no longer pitiful! See, I'm the new D.A. who will probably be seeing you soon in the courtroom when your husband goes to trial for embezzling from Exxon/Mobile. Uh-huh. Yes, that would be me. I've crawled right across those tracks that use to separate us. So, a little advice. Before you trash someone, make sure you know that they can't send your husband up the river for five to ten years. Because that would be pitiful! Good to talk to you too, Morgana. I'll see you in church. Bye now.

BOOTY CALL

Character: Sharron
Age: 30s – 50s

Scene Synopsis: SHARRON walks with great effort, carrying her phone and a cup of tea. She has a black eye and possibly a swollen face.

SHARRON

Well, I can barely move, but I made a difference, Jayne. And that's important to me at my age. Well, I beat up a wife-beater who was dragging his wife, kickin' and screamin' down a sidewalk, but not before he used me as a punchin' bag. That poor pitiful woman watched me beat her husband with a umbrella, while she was shiverin' like a scared Chihuahua in my Range Rover. I left him in the street, spitting teeth and blood and I am very proud of that.
(pause)
But—the entire story is embarrassing as hell. Well, the heroic moment of the ordeal is not embarrassing, but me gettin' to that heroic moment… well… I've never been that good of a liar and I tried to make something up, but why would anybody in their right mind drive over to Oak Cliff? What am I gonna say – that I was looking for good barbecue – at one o'clock in the morning? Okay, if you must know, but this is to the grave, Jayne Patricia West! To the grave!
(pause)
It was a booty call. Yes, I drove to Oak Cliff to get laid by some big, muscle-bound, black man I met on the internet named Dimetre. Couldn't have been more than thirty years old and had a…
(whispers)
… penis as big as my arm!
(pause)
He sent me a picture of it is how I know. They call them "dick shots". Why the hell do you think I would risk my life and drive over to Oak Cliff in the middle of the night!? Certainly not to get laid by some middle-aged white man like Jake with a shriveled up pencil dick that doesn't work except with Viagra!

(pause)
Oh don't you judge me. I know he's your brother and I'm sorry if that was awkward, but don't you dare judge me! Not after your four marriages and that affair you had with a UPS woman!
(chokes up)
And especially not after what your brother put me through. Don't you dare judge me, sister!

STOLE

Character: Penelope
Age: 40s – 60s

Scene Synopsis: PENELOPE is standing in a fur stole, dressed almost period, old money, in front of a wine wall in her beautiful home. She is on the phone with her best friend Barbara.

PENELOPE

It is missing! Gone! Vanished! Now you do the math, Barbara. A two thousand dollar bottle of Screaming Eagle is just missing! Three people in my home since I saw it last. Lula Belle who has never stolen from me and is a Hard Shell Baptist who doesn't drink at all... LeRoy was an alcoholic and died in that unfortunate tractor accident. Drunk as Cooty Brown drivin' farm equipment. Not smart. No way it was Lula Belle. Oh, and by the way, thank you very much for recommending the worst movie I've seen in decades - The Help! Please, Barbara, that movie makes white people look stupid and bad. I mean, who in their right mind couldn't taste human defecation in a pie?! I don't care how much cocoa, butter and sugar you put in it! That is a racist movie! Against good Christian white people. I told Lula Belle not to see it. Might give her some ideas. So, anyway, Mama came over on Friday, but she does not need to steal. With her old money entitlement, she'd just say, "I'm taking this!"
(pause)
And then there's that almost midget Claudine Hopkins who has more money than God but is a G.D. clepto. Tammy Faye Baker was a clepto, you know? Oletta Jacobs said that Claudine once stole a crystal cup from her mama's punch bowl set. Right after playing Bridge, Oletta was seeing Claudine to the front door and spotted that cup sitting in her Louis Vitton open purse with ginger ale and lime sherbet foam still on the rim. And she couldn't even confront her! I wouldn't snatched that cup right out that almost midget's hand, then snatched her bald headed! I know it was her. Process of elimination. A known clepto, Episcopalian, almost midget who could reach my two thousand dollar

bottle of Screaming Eagle. I'm hangin' up right now and calling the law!
Bye, bye.
(hangs up, redials)
Yes, I need to report a crime!

FOURTH BEST FRIEND

Character: Kindall
Age: Youth – Teens

Scene Synopsis: KINDALL is on the phone, not happy.

KINDALL
Oh no, she did not! She did not! Oh no, she did not!!!
(pause)
Okay, listen to me, because you're her best friend and you're my third... No fourth best friend.
(pause)
Claire, Macy and Rachel... then you! Yes, Rachel over you because she loaned me her Louis Vuitton purse for my grandmama's funeral. One of the saddest days of my life and she came through for me, Becca. Sorry. So, I temporarily bumped her up, okay? Two weeks... no three... then you'll be number three again, but only if you tell that little, lyin' crazy, boy-stealin' biach Leanna Minton that I am done with her. Done! I am done! She knew I had a crush on Taylor Parker and you do not move in on my man.

LONG DISTANCE

Character: Megan
Age: 20s – 30s

Scene Synopsis: Megan is standing at the island eating ice cream. She is in sweats and a t-shirt on the phone.

MEGAN
Oh, well... I'm just laying here in bed, completely naked... well, I do have high heels on. You know, the silver ones that I wore to your brother's wedding. And... I'm rubbing my tits while you're... oh yeah... Um-hum, that's it. And now... well, I'm fingering myself... just feeling your huge cock inside me, oh, baby... yes... pound me... love me... harder, yes, harder... deeper, yes, yes... oh, yes, yes... more... more... that's it... oh baby, you are... so... so...
(pause)
Did you come?
(mouths)
Thank God.
(pause)
Yeah, me too. It was so great. The best. Almost like you were here. I love you too. Call me tomorrow.
(hangs up, continues to eat ice cream)

NAMING DEAD FROGS

Character: Florence

Age: 40s+

Scene Synopsis: FLORENCE DOUGLAS is a high school teacher. She sits at her kitchen table with papers around that are being graded. She stares at her address book, phone in hand, makes a decision and dials.

FLORENCE
Hello, Louise. Louise Rollins? Yes, this is Florence Douglas. How are you this evening?
(pause)
Well, I'm fine… but… well, there is a pretty serious matter that I need to discuss with you.
(listens)
Yes. Well, as you know, Graham is in my biology class, doing okay, not great… and it's that time of year where we dissect dead frogs. Well… now… your son… well, Louise, you know that that boy is, well, different, and… okay – This afternoon, I passed out the frogs… and Graham… he asked if he could name his frog.
(pause)
Yes, Louise, that's right. He wanted to name a dead frog floating in formaldehyde that he was about to slice open with a blade. Louise, now, I have never been the type of educator that suppresses a child's imagination and creativity, I actually encourage that… but, Louise… Graham, your son, when he named his frog… he named it… Pat Mc-Crotch.
(pause)
Say it slowly and you will most definitely "get it". Pat. My. Crotch!
(reacting, upset)
Louise, I need you to stop laughing! This is not a laughing matter.
(waits a minute)
Thank you. So, I told him that he had to rename his frog and you know what he blurted out? He said, your son said, "Then his name is Phil

McGroin"! Louise! Stop laughing! This is not funny! His lab partner is Missy Davis and her family are devout Christians… daddy is a deacon over at Emmanuel Baptist… and trust me, they were not amused.
(pause)
Louise, I need you to stop laughing. Okay, then…I tell you what. You pull yourself together, then call me back! Goodbye!
(hangs up)

ABOUT THE AUTHOR

Photo by Jason Grindle

DEL SHORES (*Writer, Director, Producer, Stand Up Comedian*) has written, directed and produced successfully across studio and independent film, network and cable television as well as theatre.

STAGE: *Cheatin'* (1984), *Daddy's Dyin' (Who's Got The Will?)* (1987), *Daughters of the Lone Star State* (1993), *Sordid Lives* (1996), *Southern Baptist Sissies* (2000), *The Trials and Tribulations of a Trailer Trash Housewife* (2003) and *Yellow* (2010). Theatre awards and nominations: Los Angeles Drama Critics' Circle, Ovation, GLAAD, Back Stage West Garland, NAACP and LA Weekly (2006 Career Achievement Award).

FILM: *Daddy's Dyin'... Who's Got The Will?* Writer/Executive Producer, (MGM), *Sordid Lives* Writer/Director/Producer (Regent Entertainment) – 13 festival Audience Awards, 3 Best Picture Awards, 1 Best Soundtrack Award. *The Wilde Girls* Writer/Director/Executive Producer (Showtime) and *Blues For Willadean* Writer/Director/Producer (Kestrel Films) – Shout Film Festival's Best Narrative Audience Award. *Southern*

Baptist Sissies (Breaking Glass Pictures)—15 festival awards, nine of them Audience Awards. Other film awards: Lifetime Achievement Award 2012 FilmOut San Diego, Emerging Artist Award 2013 Stanley Kramer Film Festival, Pioneer Filmmaker Award 2014 B'more QFest,

TELEVISION: *Ned and Stacey*, *Dharma and Greg*, *Queer As Folk* Writer/Executive Producer and *Sordid Lives: The Series* Writer/Director/Producer.

STAND-UP NATIONAL TOURS: *Del Shores: My Sordid Life* (2010), *Del Shores: Sordid Confessions* (2011), *Del Shores: Naked.Sordid.Reality* (2012), *Del Shores: My Sordid Best* (2013-2014), *Del Shores: SINgularly Sordid* (2015-2016), *My Sordid Life, Sordid Confessions* and *Naked. Sordid. Reality.* have been released on DVD.

Del is represented by Bradley Glenn at The Kaplan-Stahler Agency as a writer-director, by Linda McAlister Talent as an actor and is managed by Michael Warwick for personal appearances. His publisher for all of his plays is Samuel French, Inc.

Twitter and Instagram @delshores. Visit and contact him via his Facebook fan page http://www.facebook.com/delshoresfanclub.

"Del Shores is the grand master of Southern sensibilities." Daily Variety

"Del Shores is a master of the Texas comedy." Los Angeles Times

Made in the USA
Lexington, KY
30 September 2016